Original title:
No One Told Me Life Was This Weird

Copyright © 2025 Creative Arts Management OÜ
All rights reserved.

Author: Penelope Hawthorne
ISBN HARDBACK: 978-1-80566-020-0
ISBN PAPERBACK: 978-1-80566-315-7

Fragments of the Peculiar

The cat wears a hat, thinks it's a king,
Dances with shadows, a whimsical fling.
Sidewalks talk back, hold secrets untold,
As squirrels throw parties, so bold and so gold.

The toaster's a DJ, spinning tunes from the bread,
Cereal sings loudly, dreams fill your head.
Umbrellas fly high, like kites on a spree,
And fish in the sea attend brunch by the tree.

Whirlwinds of the Uncommon

Penguins in pajamas parade through the street,
With ice cream for lunch and a dance that's elite.
Clouds wear the colors of funky tie-dye,
While chickens in goggles wish they could fly.

Time skips like stones over lakes of surprise,
My watch has a mustache, it opens its eyes.
Llamas in limousines zoom past with flair,
Disco balls twinkle, float high in the air.

Eccentricities of Existence

A bicycle sings as it rides down the lane,
With candy-floss wheels, it's gone just like rain.
Ducks wear tuxedos, play chess on the grass,
While ghosts throw a bash that's a right bit of class.

Mirrors reflect dreams, not faces, it's true,
Like socks that decide they're a dance crew for two.
The moon tells the jokes at the midnight café,
And socks on the floor have begun to ballet.

Threads of the Incomprehensible

Bananas in suits debate life with great zest,
While elevators giggle; they know they're the best.
The fridge holds a concert, with leftovers in tow,
As pillows decide it's time for a show.

The carpet's a runway where slippers can strut,
And umbrellas giggle when sunshine's a nut.
Time dances backwards, in a tutu so bright,
While stars play hopscotch in the warm summer night.

Chronicles of the Unusual

A cat in a hat, it walked by me,
Sipping tea, oh so nonchalantly.
Fish fly high, on a sunny day,
Jellybeans dance, in a curious way.

Pigs in tuxedos, taking a ride,
On skateboards made of broccoli, side by side.
Seven-legged spiders weave a tune,
Underneath a glowing, purple moon.

When Reality Twists

I tripped over a cloud, soft as a sigh,
And found talking squirrels who asked me why.
Bread that sings and butter that glows,
In kitchens where spaghetti wriggles and flows.

Elevators that dance to a jazzy beat,
While teacups gather for a tea-party meet.
Peacocks in spectacles, wise and keen,
Discussing life like it's all a dream.

Collisions with the Strange

A pogo stick that jumps at the speed of light,
While rubber ducks argue, in mid-flight.
My goldfish recites poetry, on a whim,
While the curtains clap hands, to join in the din.

Cactus wearing glasses, reading a book,
And noses that whistle if you take a look.
Umbrellas that chat when it starts to rain,
Making fashion statements, with no hint of shame.

The Curiosities of Existence

A pickle on a skateboard, cruising along,
Sings a tune that's delightfully wrong.
Sunflowers gossip about bees in the hive,
Unraveling secrets, just trying to thrive.

Cats wear sneakers and jog down the street,
While the moon throws a party with stars for guests sweet.

Bananas debate if they're fruit or not,
In a world so bizarre, we question the plot.

Gleams of Absurdity

In a world where socks go solo,
And cats run for office, it's quite a show.
Bananas might tango with hats on their heads,
While bread sings a ballad to lost crusty breads.

A fish wrote a novel, don't ask how it's done,
It's all in the waves, it thinks it's great fun.
Pies float on clouds and giggle out loud,
Their crusts wearing sunglasses, proud and unbowed.

Ephemeral Echoes of the Strange

Umbrellas turn into jellyfish on the street,
They wave at the wind, so light on their feet.
Mirrors hold parties for faces they steal,
While bicycles debate how to feel real.

A frog sings a tune that the crickets must dance,
As jellybeans plot their next great romance.
Cacti wear hats and share sassy remarks,
In the land where the fireflies flicker like sparks.

Quests into the Unknown

A treasure map drawn on a pizza box wide,
X marks the spot where the anchovies hide.
Mountains of marshmallows, rivers of cream,
Pirates who skateboard and sailors who dream.

The toast comes alive with a dance that's absurd,
While teapots discuss the last thing they heard.
Chasing the shadows where giggles reside,
Sailing through clouds on a fish-shaped ride.

Chronicles of the Curious

A walrus in glasses reads books by the shore,
While goosebumps on turtles tell tales of yore.
Ice cream cones whisper sweet nothings at night,
Under the gaze of a disco ball light.

Raccoons in tuxedos, planning a ball,
Invite all the kitchenware, oh what a haul!
Toaster gets jealous, and fries start to fry,
As spatulas waltz, and the napkins all sigh.

The Absurdity of Everyday

I woke up this morning, socks don't match,
My coffee's a dance, it's hard to catch.
The cat's in the fridge, the dog's on the chair,
Is this reality, or just a fair share?

The traffic's a circus, honks like a tune,
A pigeon on roller skates, under the moon.
The world spins in circles, glitter and glue,
Just laughing at life, like we often do.

Jigsaw Puzzles in the Mind

With thoughts like puzzles, scattered and bright,
Where pieces are missing, still feels just right.
The cat's got my keys, my phone's in the cake,
A puzzle to solve – just for fun's sake.

Backwards and sideways, it spins and it sways,
Logic takes coffee breaks for days.
I ask for some answers, they giggle and tease,
While ducks in suits make deals with the breeze.

When Normality Takes Leave

Normal left town on the last train out,
Leaving oddities dancing, without a doubt.
My neighbor talks to shadows on the wall,
While robots play poker in the hall.

Giraffes on bicycles, racing at noon,
Oddball conventions under the moon.
As reality takes a holiday spree,
Laughter erupts, setting us free.

Laughter in the Shadows

There's chuckles in corners and giggles in cracks,
The light has its own peculiar hacks.
As shadows recite their own silly skits,
The walls hold their breath, just waiting for fits.

I often find humor in socks with a twist,
A banquet for smiles that can't be missed.
Life throws us a party, confetti and glee,
In the weirdness of life, we just let it be.

Portraits of the Unconventional

In a world where cows wear shoes,
And waffles dance with syrup hues,
A cat that speaks in rhymes all day,
Makes normal seem a little gray.

The mailman rides a unicycle,
While squirrels plot a grand revival.
With tea parties held by the trees,
Laughter echoes on the breeze.

A fish that tells the weather news,
And poodles sporting vibrant blues,
Life stretches far beyond the norm,
In a realm where all is warm.

So here's to quirky little ways,
That brighten all our mundane days.
Embrace the odd, the strange, the fun,
As life's a dance—we've just begun.

Whimsy in the Mundane

The toaster sings a morning tune,
While socks prepare to leave the room.
A fridge that whispers secrets hear,
Transforming breakfast into cheer.

A mailbox with a quirky grin,
Collects the bills like a violin.
And curtains have begun to sway,
In waltzes through the light of day.

With jellybeans that leap and play,
And flowers that have much to say,
Every corner holds a jest,
In this peculiar little quest.

So skip along the crooked path,
And greet the silly with a laugh.
For ordinary holds a glow,
In moments we have yet to know.

Footprints in the Weirdness

The dog wears sunglasses at the park,
And whispers jokes to those with spark.
While turtles breakdance on the grass,
Challenging each other to outclass.

My neighbor paints their house bright pink,
And serves up cakes that throw you a wink.
A tree that shimmies in the breeze,
Displays a smile with utmost ease.

The mailbox sprouted legs last week,
And now it roams, so bold, so cheek!
While crayons hold a protest meet,
Declaring colors can't be beat.

In life's odd footprints, we shall tread,
With hearts so light and minds widespread.
So let's embrace the quirks, the flair,
For in this weirdness, joy's laid bare.

Curved Reflections of Existence

A mirror shows a dancing cat,
Wearing shoes and chasing that.
As rainbows hide behind the rain,
And doughnuts float on thoughts insane.

The clock has hands that twist and shout,
While clouds join in the silly rout.
Bananas climb to reach the pie,
And giggles sprinkle through the sky.

The sun plays hide-and-seek at noon,
While rabbits juggle with a spoon.
In every crevice, laughter grows,
In this wild life, anything goes.

So let's embrace each strange surprise,
And paint our dreams in vibrant dyes.
For life's a canvas, wild and free,
With curves of joy for you and me.

The Jigsaw of the Surreal

Pigeons wear tiny hats, so chic,
While squirrels plot their next critique.
The moon dances, full of glee,
As cats recite poetry with tea.

Raindrops fall in slow-motion rain,
A dog pursues his own tail train.
A clock ticks backwards, what a sight!
Yet all feels perfectly, strangely right.

Cucumbers gossip about the sun,
In fields where all the ghosts just run.
Whimsical shadows play on walls,
And laughter echoes through the halls.

Fractured Realities

My toaster sings a morning song,
While socks engage in battle strong.
Carrots wear glasses, reading cake,
In a world where fish learn to skate.

The floor tap dances, oh what fun,
As elephants have races, on the run.
A pickle whispers secrets sweet,
And all my worries take a seat.

Spiders weave tales of daring days,
While chairs do yoga in playful ways.
The grass is blue, the sky is green,
In this bizarre and joyful scene.

Vignettes of the Unexpected

A fork believes it's from a band,
While spoons rehearse a magic hand.
The fridge recites Shakespeare in the night,
And wall clocks giggle at the plight.

Pillows float like clouds in dreams,
As jellybeans strategize their schemes.
A vacuum hums a lively tune,
To serenade the sleepy moon.

Candles debate who's more bright,
While pillows practice for a fight.
The curtains dance with joyful flair,
In a world that's wonderfully rare.

The Joy of the Strange

Lemons wear ties, sprucing up a show,
While light bulbs whir with ideas aglow.
A bicycle juggles while on two wheels,
And sandwiches debate their own meals.

Bicycles ride themselves at dusk,
Under trees that talk of ancient husk.
Spring flowers gossip about the bees,
And spoons dream of sailing the seas.

Cats play chess with pieces of cheese,
While the wind giggles, doing as it please.
Life's sweet quirks abound in this strangeness,
In laughter we find our deepest freshness.

The Anomaly of Solitude

In a room full of chatter, I sip my tea,
Wondering why I'm so lonely and free.
Talking to plants, they offer no views,
But at least they won't judge my strange shoes.

I tried to find friends in the fridge one night,
The pickles agree, but the mustard won't bite.
A dance with the fridge door, so awkward and neat,
In this solo ballet, I'm my own beat.

Fables from the Fringe

A squirrel once sought to be king of the trees,
He wore a fine crown made of nuts and of cheese.
His court? A parade of confused little ants,
They plotted great feasts and choreographed dances.

The owl gave a hoot, 'You're all so absurd!'
As the rest just sat back, munching crumbs, undeterred.
This tale of a kingdom, both silly and grand,
Taught me that weirdos can really be bland.

Life's Unscripted Adventures

Booked a flight to nowhere, the pilot just grinned,
Told me to sit back; the fun was about to begin.
We flew through a sunset, dipped into a cloud,
Turns out the passengers were all just too loud.

Landed in a town known for upside-down shoes,
Everyone walks like they're stuck in a snooze.
I joined in their shuffles, felt light on my feet,
Step by step, I replicated defeat.

The Oddity of Choice

I chose between pizza and a pie made of flies,
The pizza was cheesy, but the flies were a surprise.
With each whim I toggled, my friends rolled their eyes,
Eating strange toppings, I wore my buffet disguise.

I could wear a tux, or go full-on in sweats,
Risky decisions come with bold internet bets.
Life's full of moments, so quirky and bright,
I flip a coin daily, just rolling for light.

The Peculiar Pathways

I woke up to a talking cat,
He offered me a hat.
I blinked once, then I blinked twice,
The world felt full of strange surprise.

The mailman danced with golden shoes,
He sang of cake, forgot the news.
A squirrel held a tiny sign,
It read, 'Here, the nuts are fine!'

The sun wore shades, like it was cool,
It played the ukulele in the school.
And every tree was having fun,
Digesting jokes, not just the sun.

As clouds would giggle, rain would fall,
I'd slip and slide down nature's hall.
With every twist, I found a delight,
In this mad, quirky day and night.

Enchanted Misadventures

A wizard sneezed a rainbow bright,
It painted trees with sheer delight.
I tripped on clouds, oh what a sight,
   A bubble bath, I took in flight.

My lunch began to sing and shout,
A pickle danced, no doubt about.
As jelly beans rapped on my plate,
   I giggled hard, this was my fate.

A dragon rode a bicycle,
With sparkly wings, it was magical.
We raced past stars, through shimmering space,
   In a world where time had lost its race.

With laughter curling in the air,
I spun in circles without a care.
For every odd thing in my way,
Brought joy and jars of laughter, hey!

The Tales of Topsy-Turvy

The moon wore socks, both stripy and bright,
It danced and twirled into the night.
A fish told jokes about a cat,
Who juggled oranges, how about that?

Upside down, the world did twist,
Cats played chess, none could resist.
A coffee cup waltzed on the shelf,
It declared, 'I drink from myself!'

Grasshoppers were all in suits,
Bargaining with tiny roots.
For every deal, a giggle ensued,
This funny place had no bad mood.

As flowers whispered silly rhymes,
I laughed out loud, counting the times.
In this topsy-turvy bliss I'd roam,
Finding joy, I felt right at home.

Peculiar Portraits of Life

The artist painted with grape juice,
A zoo of animals, oh what a use!
A hippo smiled, a lion too,
Strange things felt like déjà vu.

The clock ticked backward, what a thrill,
As jelly beans spilled down the hill.
Each step I took, I met a stranger,
A talking tree, but no real danger.

In this gallery of the odd,
A sandwich bowed, quite like a god.
With mustard flair, it took a stand,
Declaring itself a mighty brand.

Oh, life's a painting, wild and bright,
With colors swirling day and night.
Embrace the weird, let giggles thrive,
In peculiar portraits, we come alive.

Whims of the Wild

In a world where ducks wear hats,
I chase behind them, full of chats.
Socks are mismatched, what a sight,
Dancing with cats under dim moonlight.

Bicycles soar on candy clouds,
While I munch popcorn, singing loud.
A statue winks, I take a bow,
Is it a prank? I just ask how.

Trees converse in whispers soft,
While squirrels play chess, all aloft.
Life's a circus, oh what fun,
Each moment a flash, like a fleeting run.

Rainbows sprinkle the afternoon,
With frogs who hum a silly tune.
Caught in the whimsy, lost in the jest,
This wild ride feels like a quest.

Journeying Through the Unfamiliar

I boarded a train with jelly beans,
A ticket from a prince of dreams.
Windows frame a bizarre show,
Past flamingos in tutus, on they go.

Maps are upside down, what a sight!
Guided by the glow of starlit night.
A compass spins, is it all a game?
Is that a dragon calling my name?

Stop for tea with a moody cat,
Who serves me scones from a worn-out hat.
Laughter echoes in unexpected ways,
Turning strangers into cabaret plays.

Through the tunnels of whimsy I glide,
With a frog as my co-pilot, oh what pride!
Each twist and turn a new surprise,
In this odd journey, life electrifies.

The Enchantment of Oddities

Whispers of ghosts in the attic high,
They play hopscotch as clouds float by.
A teapot sings a lullaby sweet,
While a bubblegum tree bears treats.

Mice in bowties declare a dance,
Each step a jump, a froggy prance.
Time ticks backward, I must confess,
The sun just wore a polka dot dress.

Sandcastles made of sparkly dreams,
Mermaids trade stories, oh, how it beams!
Their laughter floats on bubbles of air,
In this world, nothing's ever fair.

Toasters toast tales of mischief and fun,
Every moment shines brighter than sun.
Oddities weave through the fabric of fate,
This enchantment stirs, and I can't wait.

Hidden Surprises Around Every Bend

Puddles are portals to worlds bright,
Where gumdrops dance in pure delight.
Snakes wear glasses, oh what a sight,
Charming the birds with their sharp wit.

Around the bend a llama sings,
Spinning tales of magical things.
A pineapple dreams of being a boat,
While a beaver writes a silly note.

Whimsical creatures complete the scene,
Bouncing on clouds in colors unseen.
Every step reveals something new,
An orange giraffe in shiny blue.

Life unfolds like a comic so grand,
With laughter and wonders hand in hand.
Hidden surprises, what's around the next?
In this odd ball, I'm forever perplexed.

Disguises of the Routine

Alarm clocks ring, but I'm already late,
Coffee mugs empty, I still contemplate.
Socks that don't match, a style of my own,
Mirror's reflection, who is that clone?

Traffic signals dance, in a puzzling way,
Cats in the window, judging my day.
A busker sings tunes that just can't be right,
I skip to the beat, it feels like a fight.

Lunch is a mystery, what's in this wrap?
Leftovers whisper, 'Join us for a nap.'
Emails like puzzles, I can't find the key,
My genius idea? Just let it be free!

Days roll like dice, each one a surprise,
Strange stains on my shirt, they're my battle cries.
Laughter erupts from a chat with my shoe,
In this circus of life, I'm the jester, it's true.

Echoes of the Unfathomable

Foggy mornings greet in perplexing glee,
Pigeons in suits fly off with my tea.
Sidewalks twist like they're in a parade,
Each step I take, a new joke is played.

Billing cycles baffle, what's that charge here?
Penguins at the mall, shopping without fear.
Conversations wander, like a lost balloon,
I nod and I smile, under the moon.

My toaster sings songs, what a funny twist,
"Have you heard the news?" it seems to insist.
I break out in laughter, it makes perfect sense,
Life's jigsaw is weird, with no recompense.

Voices from the fridge whisper secrets of old,
Magic in the mundane, I'm happy and bold.
Waking up to find a face in my bread,
This slice of existence, well, here goes my head!

Shadows of the Surreal

Waltzing with shadows in the late afternoon,
The sun throws a party, the sky's out of tune.
Chairs knock and chatter, like they've gone mad,
A lighthearted chaos that makes me feel glad.

Whispers from bookshelves, giving me plots,
Can a cactus be my therapist? (Why not?)
Timers that tick, but they're running in place,
All of this nonsense, yet I find grace.

Puddles reflect, distorted and shy,
Fish wear top hats, waving as they fly.
Sidewalks are tightropes, I teeter and sway,
A balancing act always leads to the play.

In dreams made of jelly, where do I belong?
A dance with the playful, a life full of song.
Each day is a riddle, wrapped up in a laugh,
Embracing the strange, I'm my own autograph.

Odd Corners of Reality

Waking up to find a sock on my cat,
He stares in confusion, what's up with that?
The fridge is a portal to snacks yet untried,
In a world that's chaotic, I take it in stride.

Dust bunnies gather, their meetings confound,
Plotting escape routes, no future is bound.
The mailman delivers a pizza instead,
It's strange how this chaos fills me with dread.

Rainbows emerge from the faucet today,
The sun's sipping coffee, unbothered at play.
Random dance parties involving my broom,
Every hour's a bonus, each moment's a boom.

Life's a jigsaw with pieces that tease,
Finding my place is a whimsical breeze.
In every odd corner, where laughter is found,
The weirdest of tales are what keeps me unbound.

Tripping on the Ordinary

I slipped on a banana peel,
While pondering the meaning of time,
It flew away like a fleeting feel,
And left me skidding in a rhyme.

Why do cats insist on staring,
As if they've seen the world unfold?
I swear they're secretly preparing,
To take over the house when I'm old.

Last Tuesday, the toaster mumbled,
I thought my bread was just shy,
But all it did was get grumbled,
As my coffee chose to fly high.

In the fridge, a pickle's plotting,
Wants to join the circus crew,
With the mustard just a-bobbing,
Proclaiming it takes two to chew.

Unexpected Currents

The universe has a funny way,
Of shifting things I can't recall,
Last week, my socks led me astray,
The right shoe's now glued to the wall.

I met a squirrel who told me jokes,
About acorns and their grand dreams,
He claimed he befriended some folks,
In a world that bursts at the seams.

Riding a unicycle in haste,
I found myself chased by a bee,
With laughter filling up the space,
How can this even be me?

Each wrong turn's a wise detour,
Life seems to giggle in delight,
For every door that's meant to lure,
Leads to more whims on a bright night.

Whispers of the Unseen

In the corner, shadows are chatting,
About my life, or so I think,
They gossip low, with tones so patting,
About the coffee spill on the sink.

There's a sock monster under the bed,
He claims he lost a shoe and a hat,
I pondered on that, filled with dread,
As I searched for my lost, fluffy mat.

Dogs in suits have strange discussions,
About the mailman and his stroll,
While I watch with quiet percussions,
Of laughter bubbling from my soul.

Butterflies dream of credit cards,
And gather secrets in their wings,
In a world that often seems hard,
Where joy flits by like silly flings.

The Absurdity of Everyday

I woke up at noon, oh sweet bliss,
Only to find that the cat's on strike,
It demands a kingdom, who could resist?
While I brew coffee—what a hike!

A chair declared, 'I'm tired of waiting',
For someone to sit and confer,
While I chuckle, my dreams conflating,
With wishes for snacks that prefer.

The fridge is an artist, it's clear,
With leftovers painted like art,
They argue about who's the best here,
Yet I'm the one playing the part.

Life's a dance, and I'm just a clown,
With mismatched socks and a big grin,
As the world spins wildly around,
With joy in chaos, let's all begin.

Confessions of the Curious

I found a sock in the fridge today,
It waved at me, then ran away.
The cat wore shades, perched on my chair,
I asked it why, it just purred in the air.

The toaster talks, or so it seems,
While I brew coffee, it shares wild dreams.
The world's upside down, let's take a ride,
With dancing spoons and a fridge as our guide.

Pigeons flap and gossip by the park,
About the squirrel who scored a big mark.
I tried to join in, but they just cooed,
And rolled their eyes, how very rude!

Yesterday's banana was quite a show,
It slipped on laughter, best move in the flow.
Life's like a carnival, full of jest,
Join the parade, it's truly the best!

The Quirkiness of Being

I wore two shoes, but one had a tale,
It offered me coffee, said, "Read the mail!"
The left sock winked, the right just sighed,
As both of them planned a great, rogue slide.

At the corner, a tree wore a hat quite grand,
It told me stories of a wandering band.
The grass giggled as the clouds did sway,
While bees danced cha-cha, no reason to stay.

My chair proclaimed it's the king of rest,
Declaring that naps are the very best quest.
With each little creak, it cackled and cheered,
In a world so odd, who could be steered?

Pizza became a poet last night, you see,
With toppings that rhymed, it was sheer jubilee.
Slice by slice, it recited its art,
In this weird life, it's a magical part!

Enigma of the Ordinary

The clock struck thirteen; what a surprise,
My tea started dancing, much to my eyes.
A plant wrote a letter, spilled all its thoughts,
About dreams of the soil and the sunshine it sought.

Meanwhile, a spoon decided to sing,
About the joy that the breakfast can bring.
The pancake flipped, and the syrup conspired,
To make mornings bright, as I admired.

Eagles play chess with the clouds in the sky,
While I ponder why my coffee won't fly.
The world spins on, with each little quirk,
Where magic meets normal, oh, what a perk!

With a wink from a worm, life's too absurd,
To miss out on laughter, the wisest word.
Embrace the chaos, don't shy away,
In this curious dance, let's laugh through the fray!

Surreal Stops on the Way

I met a cactus who wanted a hug,
It just stood there, both smirking and snug.
A sunflower offered me sandwiches nice,
With pickles and laughter, a peculiar slice!

The moon in the mirror winked at my feet,
Said, "Life's a riddle, come take a seat!"
Shoelaces tangled in a grand old debate,
As I stuck my tongue out, feeling first-rate.

A duck in a bowtie was selling fine hats,
While pondering life with two philosophical cats.
They sipped on tea, spoke of stars on parade,
In this amusing realm, all sanity swayed.

On my way home, I tripped on a tune,
That danced through the air, all the way to the moon.
Each step had a giggle, a bounce in my heart,
In this silly journey, I'll never depart!

Remarkable Revelations

I saw a cat wearing a hat,
It strutted like a king!
The bird nearby laughed so loud,
It gave my heart a zing.

A dog tried to chase its own tail,
Round and round it spun!
I pondered life's little quirks,
And chuckled at the fun.

A fish wore goggles in the pond,
Who knew they loved to swim?
Each day's a page of nonsense,
With laughter as the whim.

I tripped on air while walking straight,
The ground just laughed with glee!
Life's a dance of slips and flips,
And pure absurdity.

The Oddly Poetic

A toaster popped the bread so high,
It soared like a new kite!
My cereal danced upon the shelf,
In morning's golden light.

Umbrellas flipped in playful winds,
As clouds began to frown.
I wore my socks upon my hands,
And ruled the funky town.

A squirrel plotted with a seed,
To conquer the great pine.
Whispers of mischief filled the air,
In every silly line.

The streetlamp blinked a secret code,
A riddle from the night.
We're all just players in this game,
Finding joy in every light.

Secrets Beneath the Surface

Beneath the waves, a clam held court,
With stars that shone so bright!
An octopus with ink like dreams,
Painted the sea in delight.

A fish wore boots and strutted proud,
Down where the bubbles play.
It winked at me, a sly old thing,
Life's tricks, oh what a display!

Coral danced like pop stars do,
In an ocean so surreal.
Each wave a burst of laughter shared,
Where oddities reveal.

A whale composed a symphony,
That echoed through the tide.
In every note, a chance to laugh,
As secrets slide and glide.

The Curious Dance of Life

A fern wore glasses, perched up high,
    In wisdom it took pride.
  It wiggled every time I walked,
    With roots that would not hide.

The sun played tag with shady trees,
    While squirrels cheered in glee.
  With every step, I questioned life,
    Just what could it all be?

An umbrella danced in the rain,
    Twisting with every breeze.
I laughed as puddles splashed about,
    Life's waltz delivers ease.

A raspberry spoke in whispers sweet,
    Of dreams it hoped to share.
Each moment's like a wacky ride,
    Filled with humor's flair.

The Flavors of the Unexpected

Life serves up flavors strange and sweet,
Like pickles in pie, a confusing treat.
One day you'll dance, the next you'll trip,
In a world full of twists, that's the fun part of the trip.

You might find a cat wearing a tie,
Or witness a giraffe learning to fly.
A talking toaster makes breakfast a show,
And rabbits in tuxes steal chocolates, you know!

Bananas in pajamas make a grand mess,
While unicorns plot a party in a dress.
Life's palette is wild, a swirling delight,
In this circus of odd, everything feels right.

When logic takes flight and reason collapses,
You'll laugh at the twists and turn into lapses.
So grab your pink socks, don them with flair,
Embrace the absurd, and have fun out there!

Serpents in the Garden of Life

In gardens where serpents wear hats and croon,
Petunias converse with the light of the moon.
Forget about apples, it's cheese that they crave,
As they slide through the grass, looking smart and brave.

A snail with a top hat is leading the pack,
While daisies debate how to get their green back.
Life's plot twists with a cheeky little wink,
Each laugh is a treasure, each sigh makes you think.

The sun throws confetti, the trees whistle tunes,
Expect the unexpected under funny balloons.
Turtles in shades pose by the pond so grand,
In this garden of whimsy, take it all in hand.

When reason sets sail on a ship made of cheese,
You'll discover great wonders with whimsical ease.
So tiptoe through laughter and dance on the grass,
In this playful tapestry, life's moments amass!

Intersections with the Curious

At corners where winks and giggles collide,
You'll find an odd shop where the strange things reside.
A dragon that knits and a crow that plays chess,
Life's peculiar puzzles can lead to success.

With sidewalks like rivers of marshmallow fluff,
And taxis that beep like they're calling your bluff.
The signs all read "Silly" in vibrant hues,
As trampolines bounce you into an amusing cruise.

Cats in sunglasses swap tales with the breeze,
Each chat filled with giggles and puzzling tease.
A piñata parade snaking down the street,
Where candy rain falls, life is quite the treat.

Sailing down laughter on boats made of dreams,
You'll find that it's fun to burst at the seams.
So take a wrong turn if it brings you a grin,
In the garden of goofy, let the adventure begin!

Wonders in the Whimsical

In lands where the silliness runs amok,
You'll see talking teapots and slippers that rock.
With flavors of laughter so sweet and absurd,
Every strange sight is a smile you've heard.

The clouds play leapfrog over rainbows and streams,
Making wishes come true with a wink and some beams.
Dinosaurs dance in a soft shoe parade,
As bees hum the tunes that the crickets have played.

A fish in a top hat gives lessons in rhyme,
While elephants walk on tightropes, sublime.
The sun wears a grin, and the moon throws confetti,
In this world of enchantment, nothing feels petty.

So pack up your giggles and wander away,
Where wonders are plentiful and whimsy will stay.
Life's a curious puzzle, both quirky and bright,
Let laughter be your guide, and embrace the light!

The Unexpected Journey Home

I left my house in a rush,
With coffee spilling all around.
The bus was late, or was it me?
Now lost, in laughter, I abound.

A cat in a hat stole my seat,
While pigeons dance a crazy jig.
I laughed so hard, I nearly snorted,
In a world where oddities dig.

The driver's karaoke style,
Made us all sing in delight.
Each stop felt like a broadway show,
Underneath the city lights.

Finally, I reached my gate,
But found I had no key in hand.
An uproar of a smirking mystery,
Was this truly what I planned?

Embracing the Eccentric

In a café with mismatched cups,
A man in shorts sings to a plant.
A penguin watches with keen interest,
While I ponder if this is a stunt.

The waitress wears a feather boa,
As she serves the soup with flair.
She says it's made of rainbow dreams,
And sprinkles magic in the air.

A juggler enters with flying pies,
Each one lands just slightly askew.
We cheer and laugh 'til our stomachs ache,
For oddities are our greatest view.

I leave a tip of jelly beans,
And skip out with a silly grin.
Each day unfolds with gentle whimsy,
In a world where quirks begin.

Tides of the Unpredictable

Waves crashing with a rhythmic clatter,
On shores where seagulls boldly prance.
A crab in shades does a funny dance,
As I stand and simply splatter.

Kites fly high like wild, mad dreams,
While children giggle in the sand.
A flip-flop flies and lands on me,
I guess that weirdness is well planned.

A dolphin joins the chaotic show,
With leaps that stir the restless sea.
I smile as I watch the tide reveal,
Life's splendid, vivid jubilee.

I gather shells of laughter bright,
And let the waves take me away.
Though life may twist like ocean foam,
I cherish every single ray.

The Surreal Sidewalk

Walking down the street today,
I met a squirrel in a tie.
He tipped his hat and said, 'Bonjour,'
And I just stood there, oh my, oh my.

A flower shop playing loud rock tunes,
As tulips bob their heads in time.
Bees breakdance, and oh, what a sight,
In this garden of rhythm and rhyme!

A traffic light is blue and green,
As I wait for a unicorn to pass.
It munches on a neon light,
In a world that's made of glass.

I stroll past a bench with rubber ducks,
Chattering as if they were wise.
I nod and wave to all my odd friends,
In a life that brilliantly defies.

Kaleidoscopes of Confusion

A cat wore glasses, oh what a sight,
Danced through the garden, in sheer delight.
Food was in colors, not meant to eat,
Pineapple on pizza, just can't be beat.

Balloons held meetings, quite late at night,
Discussing the merits of a moonlit flight.
Socks became politicians, what a grand turn,
Voting for stripes until they could burn.

The toaster sings ballads while toasting bread,
With jellybean dreams that dance in your head.
Chickens wear hats, they sashay with flair,
While pancakes practice their breakdancing air.

So tip your hat to the strangeness around,
In wonders of whimsy, we're all tightly bound.
Life's only a puzzle, a curious game,
With twists and turns, never quite the same.

The Language of the Absurd

Penguins in tuxedos walk down the lane,
Reciting Shakespeare on a tiny train.
Pigs in the parlor, they serve up tea,
While the goldfish debates philosophy.

A hedgehog plays chess with a rabbit so wise,
Critiquing the moves, both humble and sly.
Lemons wear glasses, they ponder the zest,
While ice cubes hold rallies to prove they're the best.

Raccoons write novels from dusk until dawn,
With plot twists involving a mystical lawn.
Mice in their micro tuxes, neatly align,
Reading bestsellers on how to be fine.

So laugh at the madness, the quirks that ensue,
In this circus of life, we're all in the queue.
Understanding the strange is quite the delight,
With jesters and jest, every day is a flight.

Wonders That Make You Blink

A cucumber dreams of becoming a star,
While coffee beans plot to travel afar.
Fish on bicycles, pedaling fast,
In a world where the weirdness is meant to last.

Jellybeans whisper secrets at night,
While donuts with sprinkles prepare for a fight.
Rain taps in rhythm on windows so wide,
While umbrellas join in, with nothing to hide.

Bubbles have parties, they float through the air,
Holding discussions on how life's unfair.
Turtles in ties, they negotiate deals,
For a chance at the wheel of a wild cart of meals.

Enchanting the daily with giggles galore,
Each moment a treasure, who could ask for more?
With whimsy and laughter, we twirl and we spin,
In this topsy-turvy world, let the fun begin!

Silhouettes of the Bizarre

Octopus dances in a top hat and cane,
Waltzing with shadows in the soft rain.
Socks have conventions, with lively debates,
On whether or not to expand their estates.

Cactus holds a concert, in the wild west,
With tumbleweeds spinning, they're never at rest.
The sun wears sunglasses, and laughs at the sky,
As clouds tell stories of how they can fly.

Flamingos build castles on cotton-candy shores,
While seagulls critique their architectural scores.
Chairs host roundtables on how to be cool,
As fish in a tux take the plunge in the pool.

So gather your giggles, let's celebrate weird,
In this carnival life, let's all be endeared.
With shadows and silhouettes, we live and we play,
In a garden of oddities, let's dance the day away.

Unraveling the Quirk

I walked a dog that barked in rhyme,
While squirrels debated the meaning of time.
A cat wore a hat and sipped on tea,
In a world where logic took a coffee spree.

A toaster is talking; it's frying my bread,
It claims that my issues are all in my head.
The fridge is a DJ, spinning tunes so fine,
While I dance in my kitchen, feeling divine.

My goldfish is swimming in loops of delight,
As it plots world domination every night.
With a wink, he proposes a heist on my snacks,
Oh, the antics of pets, they cut no slack!

In this groove of oddity, I find my peace,
Where normalcy's banished, and laughter won't cease.
I toast to the quirky, the weird, and the wild,
For in this strange circus, I remain a child.

Whispers of the Abnormal

A tree starts to giggle, its branches a sway,
As I trip over roots that decide to play.
A shadow once whispered, 'Life's quite absurd,'
And I nodded along, as if it had heard.

The clouds gossip loudly, trading their shapes,
While I chase after rainbows and hope they'll escape.
A beetle in bowties insists he's the king,
He rules over puddles, such whimsical bling!

Frogs leap like dancers on lily-pad stages,
Reciting old tales with exaggerated pages.
The sun takes a break, for an afternoon nap,
While the moon writes a novel on the edge of a map.

In this carnival of odd, I find my grace,
Every glance and each smile's a curious embrace.
With a heart full of laughter, I march on ahead,
Through the whispers of life with dreams in my head.

Dancing with the Unexpected

A penguin in shades slides down my street,
He's moonwalking and grooving on flippers and feet.
With a wink and a twirl, he invites me to dance,
In this wild little world, we twirl in a trance.

The sky grins like candy, bright colors collide,
While the ducks wear top hats, waddling with pride.
A rainstorm of giggles, umbrellas abound,
With a twist and a shimmy, I spin 'round and 'round.

A cake starts to sing while it waits on a plate,
Its frosting declares, "I'M your dessert fate!"
With sprinkles as confetti, we join in the fun,
Each slice is a smile; out in the sun.

In this dance of the strange, I take my chance,
To laugh with the quirky, a most joyous dance.
For in every odd moment, I find my refrain,
Embracing the weird like a soft, sweet refrain.

Chronicles of Unseen Happenstance

The toaster's a philosopher, preaching with crumbs,
While socks hold a summit for lost, wandering chums.
Each corner I turn brings a new escapade,
Where shadows and light seem to have a parade.

A frog on a unicycle spins tales of delight,
Of missed opportunities under moonlight.
And the goldfish roll their eyes like they know,
The secrets of life like a Broadway show.

A cat in a bowtie writes poems with flair,
While plotting the overthrow of my comfy chair.
With gusto, it leaps, oh, the drama unfolds,
In this land of the weird, where lunacy holds.

In these chronicles strange, a smile is the key,
For laughter and oddity make me feel free.
With each quirky adventure, I cherish each spin,
In this merry-go-round where the fun can begin.

Serendipity's Mischief

Dancing shoes on the wrong feet,
Puddles jump when I'm on the street.
Cats wear hats, while dogs play chess,
Every moment's a funny mess.

Lemonade tastes like pickle juice,
Trees are gossiping, what's the excuse?
Socks disappear in the washing spin,
Clocks melt slowly, where do we begin?

Grocery carts have their own plans,
Pickles strut like they're in bands.
The sun winks at the passing clouds,
Laughter sings in the bustling crowds.

Each day brings a curious surprise,
Like dancing llamas in fancy ties.
Life's a jester, full of glee,
Embrace the odd, just let it be.

A Carnival of Oddities

Colors collide in a spinning wheel,
Marshmallows float, what's the deal?
Talking flowers burst into song,
In this circus, we all belong.

Balloons drift with a secret plan,
Though spiders often play in a band.
Cotton candy clouds come to play,
Wishing stars trip over their sway.

Frogs wear ties, and pigeons too,
The world's quite odd, but who knew?
Every corner has something funny,
Laughter echoes, sweet as honey.

We ride roller coasters made of dreams,
In a land where nothing's as it seems.
Hop on the ride that never ends,
Where every twist is a joy that bends.

When Reality Twists

Mugs of coffee wink with delight,
As rainbows dance in the fading light.
Kites are tangled in the tree's embrace,
While squirrels race with a silly grace.

Time takes a leap, then does a spin,
Chasing shadows with a goofy grin.
Jellybeans bounce on the kitchen floor,
Each jump is like a riddle's score.

Windows laugh at the passing street,
Candy canes melt, bittersweet.
A twist of fate in the silliest way,
Scratch your head, what did they say?

Life's a puzzle, let's play it right,
With giggles echoing through the night.
Reality's a prankster, take it in stride,
And ride the waves of a whimsical tide.

Mosaics of the Peculiar

A jigsaw made of mismatched dreams,
Fish on bikes, or so it seems.
Umbrellas dance in the breezy air,
All join in—who really cares?

Pancakes flip, singing their tune,
While shadows swirl beneath the moon.
Questions parade in colorful dress,
With a wiggle and giggle, they confess.

Crayons argue, picking their favorite hue,
Politics debated by the kangaroo.
Life's an art gallery, wild and free,
Paint it odd, that's the key!

Mosaics crafted from laughter's spark,
Scatter joy in each tiny mark.
Let's dance through the quirks that we find,
For the strange is simply life unconfined.

Rippled Reflections

In a puddle, I saw a dream,
Dancing ducks, or so it seemed.
They waddle by, give me the eye,
As if to say, 'Come give it a try.'

The clouds once wore a silly hat,
A rainbow sprouted, how about that?
Each twist and turn in life's grand show,
Is like my sock, where did it go?

My breakfast spoke in muffled tones,
As I debated with my scones.
An egg whispered, 'Don't eat me whole,'
But the toast just laughed; it took a roll.

The cat danced round in a paper bag,
While my thoughts did an awkward drag.
Life's circus tent is pitched so high,
Where laughter's the truth in the sly goodbye.

Serendipity in Shadows

A true magician pulls from the dark,
A lizard with a tiny spark.
It leaps around like it knows the game,
In a world where nothing's really the same.

The moon forgot to wear its clothes,
Poking out in a pair of poses.
With giggles hiding in midnight air,
Every shadow has a secret to share.

My coffee dreams of being a latte,
While sugar plays shy, a sweet ballet.
The spoon taps out a lively beat,
In the kitchen, where oddities meet.

In the corner lurks my lost shoe,
Claiming it's having a barbecue.
And as I chase my whimsical fate,
I trip on laughter—oh, isn't it great?

Labyrinths of the Unexpected

A box arrived, all wrapped in tape,
Contained a sock, or maybe a cape.
I pondered deep, scratching my head,
What kind of wizard is stirring in red?

The dog found a hat, now thinks it's grand,
Strutting about like he's in a band.
Each twist and turn has made me flee,
For who knew sneezes could dance with glee?

A sandwich sang a wobbly tune,
As jelly beans jumped at the full moon.
Ketchup offered a winking smile,
In this puzzle where logic takes a while.

Life's a riddle, wrapped up in fun,
Each mishap sparking laughter's run.
Through every corner of this maze,
Is it madness, or a wacky craze?

Epiphanies at Odd Hours

The clock strikes twelve, what's that sound?
A potato rolling 'round and 'round.
It giggles loud, whispers 'don't sleep,'
Exploding truths that make me leap.

The cat's plotting a party tonight,
With shadows swirling in soft moonlight.
And as I try to grasp this scene,
The fridge hums low, as if it's keen.

The flowers debate who's the best,
While ants declare, 'We are the quest!'
Each petal's gossip sends me off track,
In the garden where time has a knack.

A slice of pizza starts to dance,
While pickle jars join in for a chance.
At odd hours, wisdom seems to hide,
But laughter is the ultimate guide.

A Symphony of Strange Encounters

A cat in a hat, what a sight,
Dancing on rooftops, taking flight.
With a parrot that sings nursery rhymes,
We stroll through puddles of jelly at times.

A bus full of llamas, oh what a show,
They wear tiny glasses, quite in the know.
While unicorns gossip about the best tea,
In a world where the normal just doesn't agree.

Why did the chicken cross the street, you ask?
To join a parade of folks in a mask.
Gumdrop unicorns prance with such flair,
Who knew sweet treats could dance in midair?

So grab all your friends, let's take a ride,
Through this land where the wacky reside.
Expect the unexpected, tide and turn,
In this quirky world, there's so much to learn.

Echoes of the Unfathomable

In the market of socks, where cucumbers talk,
The fish wear bowties, they're ready to rock.
A penguin with flair strolls in with a shoe,
Winking at chickens in vibrant hues.

What's that sound? A clock that is singing,
As frogs on stilts do their own flinging.
A riddle from rabbits, eat carrots for brains,
In a world where logic just wears silly chains.

Lemonade rivers flow through candy fields,
Where mushrooms give pep talks, their wisdom reveals.
Balloons can't stop dancing under the sun,
As laughter erupts and the merry-go's run.

So twirl with the odd, let your spirit be free,
In this bizarre realm, embrace the glee.
With echoes that ring, laughter fills the air,
Join in the chorus, let's all be aware!

The Road Less Ordinary

On a road paved with gumdrops and dreams,
A snail spins a tale, or so it seems.
Traffic jams caused by marching bands,
As rain falls up in these shifting sands.

A bubblegum bridge leads to nowhere fine,
With a sign that reads, "Join the dance line!"
A sock puppet mayor holds a debate,
On whether or not to dance on a plate.

The clouds wear pajamas, fluffy and bright,
Tickling the trees, what a whimsical sight.
With stars playing hopscotch in a moonbeam glow,
Adventure awaits where no ordinary goes.

So pack up your quirks, let's hit the trail,
With giggles and quirks, we'll prevail.
Life's a melody sung out of tune,
In a tale that makes you swoon like a cartoon!

Curiosities of the Heart

Why does my heart wear mismatched shoes?
It dances to rhythms, sings bright blues.
In the garden, I found a talking tree,
Whispering secrets of who I could be.

A heart-shaped pancake flipped just for fun,
As squirrels throw confetti and everyone runs.
With dreams made of jelly and hopes in a jar,
We collect all the wonders, wish on a star.

A wild idea bloomed in a toaster this morn,
Sprouting giggles like popcorn corn.
With each quirky thump, our spirits collide,
In this odd little journey, let's take it in stride.

So treasure each beat, let your laughter unfold,
In this book of odd tales waiting to be told.
With curiosities fluttering, let's dance in delight,
In a heart that is weird, we find our own light.

Encounters in the Bizarre

In the park, a dude in a cape,
Feeding squirrels with a crepe.
Two dogs argue over a shoe,
Is this real or just a preview?

A cat in glasses reads a book,
While the goldfish gives me the look.
Around the corner, a chicken struts,
Wearing boots, oh what a fuss!

A man on stilts plays hopscotch,
While pigeons plot a grand debauch.
I laugh and wonder, is this fate?
Or just my mind on a wild date?

Bicycles float in the sky,
As I question the reasons why.
Perhaps it's all a cosmic joke,
That makes me grin with every poke.

Dancing with the Unpredictable

A fish that can tap dance quite well,
Spins around in a water swell.
The moon winks as I take a chance,
And join the stars in a silly dance.

A llama winks, then starts to prance,
Twirling 'round, it's quite a chance.
I toss my shoes to the grass below,
And follow its lead in the glow.

The trees start clapping, birds join the tune,
As shadows streak under a silver moon.
I laugh aloud, forgetting the rest,
In this mad ballet, I feel so blessed.

A puddle bursts into a giggly song,
As we all dance, it can't be wrong.
Reality bends, and doubts disappear,
In this mad world, I've found my cheer.

Juxtaposed Journeys

A snail dreams of racing a hare,
But finds itself tangled in hair.
A turtle claims, 'I've got a plan!',
As it zooms past a speeding van!

In a cafe, I spot a giraffe,
Sipping tea, doing math by half.
My coffee spills in a magic swirl,
As a squirrel starts to twirl and twirl.

A mime practices under the sun,
Caught in a box, while I share the fun.
A dog delivers my lunch with flair,
I'm left in stitches, thoughts everywhere.

A robot juggles with great finesse,
While I ponder my own success.
In a world so wonky, absurd yet bright,
The joy of oddities fills my night.

Marvels in the Mundane

At the grocery, clouds whisper and laugh,
While a banana tries to take a bath.
Sarcastic carrots gossip and glare,
While I stand still, without a care.

The carts dance in their own parade,
As I watch in awe, totally swayed.
The milk jugs wobble with teasing grace,
And the bread rolls race to get a place.

In my dreams, socks have their own style,
Debating on which should go for a mile.
Jelly beans break into chatter and song,
And dancing cupcakes can't help but belong.

A world within a mundane stroll,
Where laughter bubbles in every role.
I stroll away with a smile and grin,
Thankful for the peculiar spin.

The Whimsy of Fate

A cat wearing socks, so dapper and spry,
Winks at a bird who just learned to fly.
The toast always lands, butter-side down,
As clowns parade through a sleepy old town.

Fish in a top hat, sipping some tea,
Speak of their plans for a grand jubilee.
The sun took a nap, but the moon stayed awake,
While jellybeans danced on the things we bake.

Palettes of the Absurd

Colors of laughter and shades of surprise,
Pandas on scooters with comical eyes.
A toast to the socks that never match right,
And bananas that argue about who takes flight.

Rainbows connect dogs that bark at the sun,
While squirrels play chess, giggling just for fun.
The clock ticks backward, it's a whimsical spree,
As marshmallows float in a sugary sea.

The Fables of Everyday Uncertainty

Teapots are singing; they have much to say,
About pickles that dance and flowers that play.
A cupcake once claimed it could run very fast,
But tripped on its frosting and fell with a blast.

Giraffes ride bicycles down the main street,
While zebras sell popcorn to kids for a treat.
In this circus of life, all the oddities gleam,
As lemons hold meetings to plan their next scheme.

Navigating the Unconventional

Search for directions in a world upside down,
Dancing with owls in a jester's old gown.
A rabbit insists it can host a grand show,
While turtles juggle pineapples, putting on a glow.

Maps drawn in crayon lead nowhere at all,
But laughter echoes through a candy-filled hall.
The daydreams are scattered like leaves in the breeze,
And logic takes naps, oh, sweet little tease.

Mismatched Moments

I woke up thinking it was Tuesday,
But it's actually Thursday today.
Wearing socks that don't even match,
My brain is lost, it's a comedy patch.

The cat is plotting with the goldfish,
They're scheming something, I can't quite wish.
The dog is staring at the wall,
As if it whispers secrets to all.

I tried to bake a cake for a treat,
But ended up with a burnt pancake sheet.
My friends all laugh as I take a bite,
Who knew my cooking could cause such a fright?

In this circus where oddballs collide,
Everyday moments take you for a ride.
With a smile, I embrace the cheer,
Who knew strange could feel so near?

The Strangeness We Embrace

The toaster pops out bread, but wait!
A sock? Oh boy, isn't this great!
I wear my clothes inside out today,
Just another twist in a typical way.

The neighbors have a goat on a leash,
It sings opera as we feast.
My phone keeps texting me 'get lost',
Maybe it's tired of the number of calls tossed?

A pigeon lands on my plate like a guest,
I offer a crumb, it laughs at my jest.
The world's a joke and I'm the punchline,
A situation that's oddly divine.

With every twist, life's not so plain,
I have my quirks, I'll always entertain.
Let's sip our tea with a wink and a shrug,
In this amusing web, we will snug.

Stumbling into the Unusual

I tripped over a garden gnome,
Thought it was a magician all alone.
It winked and waved, I must have dreamed,
But everything's strange, or so it seemed.

The spaghetti danced on my plate tonight,
I chuckled, thinking it had taken flight.
Noodles don't jiggle, but here we go,
With each twirl, what a curious show.

A bird in a hat sings with flair,
While I sip coffee in my armchair.
I thought about joining this whimsical band,
But my feet seem stuck like they're made of sand.

Life's a carnival, spinning so fast,
Each stumble and fumble makes laughter last.
With every oddity and laugh that appears,
I embrace the quirks and face all my fears.

The Charm of the Unexpected

A banana slipped right under my feet,
Sending me tumbling, oh what a feat!
A laugh from the crowd, and I stand up tall,
Life's a comedy show; I'm giving it my all.

I opened the fridge to say 'what's for dinner?'
A disco party? I've never been thinner!
Dancing veggies with a rhythm so bold,
They moved with a groove that never gets old.

A lawn flamingo stares with a grin,
Who knew such fun could come from a spin?
With every bizarre twist that comes my way,
I find the delight in the laugh of the day.

So let's raise our glasses to the odd and the fun,
In this topsy-turvy world, we can run.
For life's little quirks bring joy to our heart,
In the playground of life, let's all take part.

Tapestries of the Unusual

In a world where socks do dance,
And cats get jobs at the finance,
Bananas wear top hats with pride,
While toasters throw parties inside.

The mailman rides a unicycle,
Delivering dreams with a smile,
Trees tell jokes that make you snort,
While squirrels plot their next cohort.

Ice cream trucks play polka tunes,
As chickens croon under the moons,
Cupcakes rain down from the sky,
And pickles launch rockets so high.

We hop on clouds made of jelly,
With our lunchboxes filled with melee,
As giggles bubble up like soda,
In the land of the quirky, we found the moda.

Echoes from the Edge

The clocks all tick backwards, they say,
And spaghetti swings like it's ballet,
Fish ride bicycles down the lane,
While turtles practice their own refrain.

Dresses made out of pancake mix,
As hamsters perform circus tricks,
Penguins in suits sell ice to the blind,
In this realm, sanity's hard to find.

Neighbors talk to their garden gnomes,
Sharing tales of far-off homes,
Jellybeans rain from a bright blue sky,
As llamas complain about why they fly.

Kites are tethered to rainy dreams,
And windows hold deep, giggling screams,
In the chaos, laugh with delight,
For everything here feels just right.

Whispers from the Peculiar

Giraffes wear shoes, it's quite the sight,
While pancakes argue who's wrong or right,
A sandwich debates life's greatest quest,
On a mustard-colored, cozy nest.

Ovens laugh while baking is done,
And crayons race just for fun,
Clouds exchange their fluff with cheer,
In a world where nonsense appears.

Dancing spoons join the fork's parade,
While apples joke beneath the shade,
Yoga mats float on rivers of tea,
In a scenery where oddity's free.

Every corner holds a surprise,
As giggles and whimsy arise,
Let's take a stroll, don't be shy,
In this realm where the strange can fly.

Adventures Beyond the Expected

Clouds are made of bubblegum,
While beetles bust out some drum,
Marshmallows bounce on pogo sticks,
In this land where nothing clicks.

The sun wears shades, sipping tea,
While frogs serenade the bumblebee,
Cactus dance in pinstripe suits,
As rabbits play jazz in jazzy boots.

Noodles swim in endless lakes,
And each wave giggles as it quakes,
Balloons chat about their keen flight,
In this realm where silly is bright.

So pack your bags with laughter, dear,
For journeys await so far and near,
In a world where whimsy reigns supreme,
Join the fun, and live the dream.

www.ingramcontent.com/pod-product-compliance
Lightning Source LLC
Chambersburg PA
CBHW051644160426
43209CB00004B/785